Paula Varjack is a writer, filmmaker and theatre maker. Her work explores identity, the unsaid, and making the invisible visible. She makes work across disciplines; performance, theatre, documentary and spoken word. Her most recent show *Show Me The Money* explores the reality of making a living as an artist in the UK based on interviews with artists across the country. She has performed at numerous arts festivals and cultural spaces including: Glastonbury Festival, Berlin International Literature Festival, Tate Modern, Chelsea Theatre, The Victoria & Albert Museum, The ICA, Richmix, Wiltons Music Hall, Battersea Arts Centre, The Southbank Centre, Círculo de Bellas Artes, Musicbox Lisbon, Es Balluard Museum of Contemporary Art, and The Photographer's Gallery.

She is the creator of *the Anti-Slam*, a satirical take on Poetry Slams where the lowest score wins. In addition to performing and producing events, she facilitates workshops with a wide range of age groups, using writing prompts and drama games to unblock creativity. Born in Washington D.C. to a Ghanaian mother and a British father, out of they many places she has lived she considers east London to be "home".

Letters I Never Sent to You

Poetry & Prose 2007–2016

Paula Varjack

Burning Eye

This edition published by Burning Eye Books 2016

www.burningeye.co.uk
@burningeyebooks

Burning Eye Books
15 West Hill, Portishead, BS20 6LG

Cover Artwork by Lauren Houston
Edited by Bram E Gieben, Robert Hill, Carys Jones

ISBN 978-1-909136-88-5

Letters I Never Sent to You

Tom,
Thank you for
the support, insight
and memories
of my father.
XX Paula

'*I have three phobias which, could I mute them, would make my life as slick as a sonnet, but as dull as ditch water: I hate to go to bed, I hate to get up, and I hate to be alone.*'

Tallulah Bankhead

To Alexandra Cooper & Meagan Crooke-King,
who I miss dearly and wish I could still see.

To Martin Bengtsson,
with whom I hope I will never stop having adventures
and collaborating.

To Ryan Nash,
who encouraged me to write poetry.

CONTENTS

PROLOGUE

What is it about questions that end in the word 'back' that always makes me feel nervous…?

Do you ever go back?

When are you going back?

How long has it been since you've been back?

For as long as I can remember, I have been travelling. I'm always leaving.

I'm always back somewhere.

Sometimes I wake up startled in unfamiliar places. I have to take a moment to remind myself where I am, why I had gone, how long I have been there.

Sometimes I travel only wanting to show you and tell you about all this, all these places and people. I wanted to share them with you. I wanted you to be there.

So I started to write to you. I wrote you stories. I wrote you poems. I wrote from every city and country I went to. I wrote to you from buses and trains. I wrote you letters in airports and planes. I couldn't stop. I wrote to you from as far as Accra and as close as the other side of the bed.

I never sent any of them. Not one. I'm not sure why.

Instead I collected them. At times I told you fragments when I saw you. But mostly I just kept them, because I wasn't sure you were ready yet.

And now you are, or maybe now I am, and here they are, all of the letters, all of the letters that I never sent.

BEGINNINGS & ENDINGS

I HAVE ALWAYS BEEN IN LOVE WITH WORDS

I'm a grown woman
and a child.
I ran before I could speak
and when those words came
thick and fast and breathless
I stopped running
and stood behind them.

When I was a child
I thought I'd be an artist.
When I was a child
I thought I'd be a writer.
When I was a child
I thought I'd be
a poet...

But that idea seemed silly
even to six-year-old me
so I changed it to
psychologist.

The circumstances that bring me here
are kind of extraordinary.
I used to refer to it
as a breakdown
but I don't know
if it was a breakdown

Maybe it's just that my fuse was burning down
slowly, insistently, determinedly.
But I like writing,
because writing is like talking.
I love talking,
but only to some people.

Talking is tricky
especially when you're the type that
talks faster than you think
and I've had a lifetime of writing
letters.

Letters that formed words,
filling ripped-up sheets of notebook paper
crinkled at the sides
where they once held fast
to spring ring binding.

Letters
delicately written on airmail paper.
Letters
typed up on crisp white card stock.
Letters,
the woman I loved who illustrated
the bottom corner of every page
with female figures
who looked me dead in the eye
as lines turned pages over.

I have always been in love with words
but I don't see them
as often as I used to.
Not on paper anyway.

The words I mix with
scroll down screens,
tumble from mouths,
trickle out of headphones,
headsets and speakers.

And I would write these words
for you to keep.
Maybe put them in a letter
and send them.
Create a new relic
fossilised with ink
and paper and stamps.

Where words fold into envelopes
and fly
on planes
like we do.

MY COUNTRY, YOU MAY HAVE HEARD OF IT

My parents moved to America at the end of the seventies. My father from England, my mother from Ghana. Yeah, yeah... no matter where you go in the world, *everyone's* heard about Ghana.

You have all these ideas from all the soap operas dubbed into your language, and teenagers everywhere listen to highlife music, wear kente' cloth, eat fufu and kelewele, imitating Ghanaian culture
to be cool.

But it's not Ghana's fault. They didn't choose to be the dominant culture. And they don't all have apartments like that in Accra. I've been there, it is kind of like the soap operas, but anyways it's my mum who's from there. I was born in this tiny city called Washington DC.

DC? Um... well, it's the capital of America.

Well, anyways:

We moved back to England when I was still a baby. England? It's in... Europe. We moved back to the States when I was five. When I was a teenager, I moved back to England. I made no great sacrifices to move... here.

I come from a relatively young country. You may have heard of it. It's called America.

I come from a very small country, you may have heard of it, it's called England. It's this small island off of Europe.

Okay. Well, I just want to know.

I mean sometimes I really wonder: what do people from all around the world think about us? When you hear *America*, when you hear *England*, what do you think of?

Have you ever even thought about England? Do you know where America is?

No, that's OK. You've never heard of it? Well, you know where Mexico is?

Yeah, yeah, yeah.

The USA is totally by Mexico, and then you know how North America is kind of shaped like…? Yeah, well, the USA is kind of the bit here.

You know?

Oh, well. Um … England, well, it's in Europe. Yeah. No, no, not that bit, that's Italy.

England is the island off the continent. It's kind of shaped like… it's next to… yeah, anyway, it doesn't matter. A lot of people haven't been. I know. You should go, the people are very friendly.

What's it like? Oh, well, we have all these rituals.

Like in my country, when you are an adolescent, there is this rite of passage called a keg party. Like in my country, when you become a young man or woman, you study at a place called uni and go on something called a pub crawl.

It is common for young men to drink pints of ale until they are so drunk they miss the last train. It is not uncommon to see young women drink alcopops and be sick outside the tube station.

Wow, it's not often someone is so interested. I am surprised you care about… I'm amazed you want to know about my country…

Why do I want to move to Berlin? Oh, well, I want to take the women. Oh, well, I want to take the men. Oh, I have no desire to integrate. But that's OK because they don't care.

My country, you may have heard of it. It's called America, it's called England.

We speak English there. Oh, you speak some English too? You learned it in school but never used it. Yeah, I guess it's not such a useful language if you're not in America, if you're not in England.

It's not so easy to learn.

In my country we learn English from a very young age. And then around age six or eight we also take English and English, and some people take English, English and English! So we all speak English and English fluently...

Maybe you can help me.

I am very much interested in moving to Berlin, Germany.

I speak no German.

But I am confident I will be qualified if applying for a job in a German company. But I don't want to have a desk job. I don't actually want to work.

We should stay in touch. Let me know if you ever decide to visit

my country.

NIGHT CHAT

We were outside smoking,
Winter hours made 4pm feel like midnight.
The countryside sky free of air and light pollution
had so many stars our urban eyes were
nearly blinded.
I exhaled wearily and said I was heartbroken
He, my friend, cast me a withering look,
said, 'Stop wasting your time with men.
You're far too clever.'
He's a sometimes feminist, part-time misogynist;
I suppose he thinks it accentuates his swagger.
My newfound interest in men has
placed me lower in status.
He maintains that I should know better
and women are far more complex
allegedly.
All I know is,
the men I'm drawn to make me crazy and
the women I'm drawn to are crazy
(so which side of clinical insanity would I like to be, I mean,
where
        does that leave me?)
I shook my head, locked eyes with him and said,
'Listen, seriously, man, I'm heartbroken.'
And the stars laughed
and the night grew darker still.
He stubbed out his cigarette and walked back in
with not so much as a word in my direction.
I think he preferred it when I was lesbian.

INVENTORY

When you walk through the front door down the hallway you will come to a closet; open it and you will see shelves and shelves of our high heels (hers are the highest). To the right, enter the living room. There is a cabinet from my parents' house; we painted it black in their back garden and inside you will find all of our CD wallets. Our books are also mixed up, in the bedroom, but we'll go in there later...

When we unpacked our boxes, our first ever argument in years of being together was about our books and CDs. She did not want to mix my books with hers, my CDs with hers. She wanted to keep her things separate. I was offended. She felt silly. So we arranged them together by type, by genre, by artist.

But where were we? Oh yes, the living room. The sofa is black leather with white piping, a two-seater. It was handmade in Brighton by a small company that specialises in art deco remakes. We went down to the shop to go through leather swatches and styles before we ordered. Next to it is a swivelling glass and chrome table, by the white leather Bibendum chair. (Not an original, but as stylish as it is comfortable. That company sent us two by accident, and we deliberated for ages as to whether we could get away with keeping the extra one.)

There is a cocktail cabinet, where my collection of martini glasses are kept, and the matching flasks we got at work, when there was a Jack Daniel's promotion at the bar. We found the dining table beside it in a tiny antiques stall in the southwest of England.

We took a train out for ages in the pouring rain to get there. The couple who sold it to us advised us how to clean it, how to prevent the surface from scratching. When we agreed to buy it we made a little toast, the four of us. They asked us about our new place; they liked us, I think; they said they wouldn't charge us to deliver.

She organised everything in the kitchen. I can never find anything but the glasses. There are red wine and white wine glasses, champagne and shot glasses, brandy balloons. All the plates, at her request, are large and white. There are heat-resistant placemats we bought at John Lewis, to protect the dining table from marks.

Walk out of the living room and down the hallway to our bedroom. There is a low dark wood double bed. We got so giggly trying out all those mattresses. The sheets white, white like the walls, the plates, the placemats.

The duvet and pillows are filled with goose down feathers. The two wardrobes and vanity are a suite from the forties. We found them on eBay, amazed at their beauty, their craftsmanship when they arrived. We liked the idea of putting on our make-up sitting at that vanity, until she finally pointed out that in that corner there was never enough light.

When it became clear it was over, for a few weeks we thought we could still live together until she found a new place, or at least we tried. And then I took a bag to a friend's place, and then she took a bag to a friend's place and she emailed me, with a tone that was exceedingly polite, asking when would be convenient for her to collect her things, asking to arrange a time.

I stayed away on the day. The next morning, when I arrived, I walked through the flat, convinced there would be something she'd forgotten, one thing she left behind. But the removal of all that was hers had been meticulous. Every CD, book, notepad, poster, card, photograph, dress, belt had evaporated from sight.

Thinking I'd catch her out, thinking I might stumble across something she had missed I looked under the beds, behind the desk, along bookshelves. But all she'd left behind was her absence, and all of the many things we had found together, chosen one by one.

THE AFFAIR BEHIND LONDON'S BACK

When I left London
we said it wasn't a break-up.
But all that
'Darling, you're the only one I ever have,
ever did, ever will'
already felt false.

I saw London yesterday;
it had been months.
It felt like years.
Our embrace was stiff.
'I miss you, when are you coming back?'
she whispered.
Coming back?
and as I wondered
my hands found familiarity in her curves,
roving but not really wanting.

I saw London yesterday;
she had that warm watery look
in those grey eyes
that I still loved
but maybe felt
less engaged by.
And her curves were too familiar.
'I miss you,'
she said again.
'I miss you too,'
I said too quickly,
placed a large wine glass in her hand
that she drank as quickly as I poured.

I saw London yesterday;
I took her out for a meal.
Candlelit… romantic.
But then Berlin walked by our table,
brushed by me
'accidentally'.
Entschuldigung.
She walked off,

25

shoulders tanned and bare.
She was glowing.

Was it from last night?
More likely this morning.
Meanwhile London was talking
about her failed attempts to give up smoking.
Berlin came up behind me,
indulgently exhaled tobacco and nicotine.
Her smoky breath danced along my neck.
I froze with how fiercely
I wanted her.

I slept with London last night
and it was good
but not great.
And I wouldn't say Berlin is a better lover
but she has this way of
getting to me.
When Berlin kisses me
she keeps one hand free,
finds my sex quickly,
eyes gleaming wickedly,
moves to another,
turns to me mouthing *join me*.

I tried to tell Berlin I had to leave.
I told her this could only be temporary.
There had been too many nights out
ending at sunrise.
Nervously I suggested
maybe we should try to take things easy?

Berlin lacht,
pleite, aber immer geil.
London had been calling, texting, Skyping, Facebooking.
I told Berlin I might be gone for a little while.
Or rather I tried to tell her
but it had been too loud in that bar.
She was ein bisschen betrunken at the open air.

She was a little occupied with that couple at the after-hour.

'I'm going,' I said.
'Stay,' she said.
Pressed several pills into my hand
and definitely didn't notice when I left.

I saw London yesterday.
She was moody.
We ended up having
make-up sex.

It was a struggle not to call out Berlin's name.
But London knows,
won't ask what I'm thinking,
feels me reconsidering.
I saw London yesterday
and all I could think about
was Berlin…

YOU COME TO A POINT

In your life you come to a point, or rather, you can come to a point… you come to a point where you take all of your worldly possessions and realise you don't really want or need any of them and then you build them up sky high and torch them, while laughing. Everyone thinks you're crazy. Maybe because you are a little. And then maybe that doesn't work either, so you decide to leave with only what you can carry and go somewhere far.

Extra points if you know next to no one, bonus points if another language is involved. Super extra bonus points if it feels like a genuine restart. And it's great really. You don't look back, you don't even think about where you've been and before you know it, you realise how much time has passed. How quickly it's passed. The wondrous hell-bent hedonism of summer, the sex, the substances, the twilight-through-daylight conversations with strangers.

The moment you realised that even though you hadn't ridden a bike since the age of fourteen, now you can ride a bike one-handed drunk in the rain while having a phone conversation, drinking a beer and smoking the cigarette that hangs from your lips. And you've been up for almost twenty hours, but you're still going to the after-hour (extra points if it's an open-air that you found out about by word of mouth).

All I knew was in my life I came to a point. A point where I fell head over heels in love with a city.

BERLIN

SIGHTSEEING

My boyfriend collects hearts…

Or rather, he takes photos of hearts. He's always finding hearts in random places. He says it's easy to find them. He says once you start looking, you see them everywhere.

After we began seeing one another, I began to notice them too. Now whenever I go to a new city, I see them. They pop up in strange places, and he's right; once you keep an eye out, they do appear everywhere.

When I was growing up, every summer my parents and I would visit my family in London. When I was little we'd always go sightseeing. When I was about eight, we (my mum, dad and grandpa) went to St Paul's Cathedral. My grandfather was about eighty then, I think. Somehow we lost my parents. We were looking up at the dome. We decided we wanted to go up there. Or maybe I decided I wanted to go up there, and my grandfather was happy to go up with me. As we were climbing up the stairs, my grandfather told me about the whispering gallery.

He said if you stood on one side of the dome, and the person you were with stood at the other side, you could whisper against the wall, and the sound of your voice would travel around to them. We went up and tried it. It's one of the fondest memories of my grandfather I have. My parents were shocked we had gone up to the top. I guess they thought I was too young, and he was too old, for all those stairs.

Today began fragile. I was painfully hungover from last night. As far as the day ahead with my parents was concerned, all I wanted was for everything to go smoothly. I asked Mum if she wanted to go to the Berliner Dom. I reminded her how much she wanted to go last year. My father and I did not complain about paying admission.

As we walked into the centre of the cathedral, my head tilted back and I looked up into the stained glass above in the dome. There was nowhere to stand up there. I guess you couldn't walk up to it.

'It reminds me of St Paul's,' Mum said.

My dad and I walked up a level, where there was a small museum. Then there were more stairs. My dad seemed bored of the cathedral by now. I told him I'd go up and check out the next level.

I walked up but there were just more stairs, and more stairs. My head was still woozy with my hangover, but for some reason I kept going. I finally saw a window above, where passing silhouettes broke up the sunlight pouring through, and then I understood. You could go up to the top of the dome, but outside rather than inside. Now all I could think about was getting up there.

There were so many stairs and little doorways, and narrow turns. You could feel the exhaustion of everyone walking in front of and behind you. It created a bond between all these strangers. Some people would take breaks and stand to the side. Doors would be held open for you as you walked ahead. Low overhangs were pointed out. By the time I reached the top, it was as if we had all achieved something together.

I looked over this city I've grown to love so much. I took a moment and paused to take it in, slowly walked around to the other side of the dome.

I thought of my grandfather and me walking up to the top of St Paul's.
I thought about all those summers I spent with my parents sightseeing.
I thought about showing my boyfriend around Berlin last summer.
I thought of him returning the favour, and showing me parts of London I'd almost forgotten.

I thought about sending him a text right then saying…

On top of a cathedral in Mitte, looking over Berlin, thinking of you.

I took out my phone.

But just as I flipped it open to write, I looked out from where I stood, and miles down on the ground below me, I saw it...

EYE CONTRACT

I didn't take you seriously.
You barely registered on my radar.
I just thought… no, actually, I didn't think anything about you.
But then the contract was set with this one glance;
I hadn't been eyed up in that way in some time.

That curious intrigued way,
that squaring-up and challenging way,
that you'd-decided-for-both-of-us way
that makes my whole body start responding
like some kind of reflex,
like a series of buttons were pressed.

Like I've been biologically programmed,
like I'm responding to unspoken commands,
when the signals are set I submit
without realising.
Our eyes were having
a very different conversation

from the one our mouths were.
You read my book
without revealing one chapter.
You played dumb
just to make me feel clever

and I thought I was coy
but my bluff was blown
when you stopped playing,
didn't wait to see my hand,
just pinned me with it against that wall
in one smooth manoeuvre,

my dress rising over my legs.
I stopped thinking altogether.
Maybe I'm a follower
who only pretends to be a leader,
all mouth until told to shut up and listen.

I was in a position

I didn't know how to get out of
and didn't really want to… either.
The last time I was in a situation like this

the contract was set with one glance
but I didn't know then that
the terms were four years
and sometimes I think
I probably should have checked
the fine print.

But this time is totally different:
the toilet cubicle replaced by a dressing room,
the town of Brighton is played by Berlin,
the bartender from Brazil is now a musician from London

And as for terms and conditions, well,
once again they were not being set by me.
I said, 'How are you so sure
that you're stronger?'
And you laughed and said,
'Because I am.'
And I didn't consider
any of the others who could have walked in.

Completely forgot about
someone else I'd been flirting with
only ten minutes before.
And there I was pinned,
a butterfly preserved,

not knowing how I'd been categorised
in my caption, and just as suddenly
as we started you stopped.
Without any explanation

let go of me
and you were walking off.
I said,

'Am I ever going to see you again?'
And you…
you just laughed.

OVERHEARD AT ST OBERHOLZ

I am. *Mega* busy. It's crazy. I don't know *where* the time goes. I have to keep up with all these Twitter posts, reading the tweets of the people I follow, retweeting the posts of the people I like, and then there are my own posts to write and sometimes it takes time to get it down to 140 characters. It involves *rewrites.*

Right... right...

Then *there's* all the news sites I read, and the gossip ones, and all of these podcasts and mixes that I download and before I get to listen to them... before I know it I'm like 'shit, I forgot about Facebook!' Not that I use it much, I just like to... *keep an eye on it,* you know? Just see what's up on my wall, and then, then there is my blog... it takes time to get right, it's my main form of expression. I mean, my blog isn't going to write itself? It's kind of like... art, right?

Right... what *do you think* of the art here?

(Sigh.) Most of the time I see art in Berlin? And I don't... *understand* it. Artists here have no incentive to *sell.* They don't need to, because they have Hartz Vier... it's all so... the art here, it's not... idealistic or conceptual it's, it's... self-entitled.

Mmm. *(Sage nods.)*

Have you thought about holding talks? I mean *consulting?*

Consulting on social media? We're thinking about it.

We thought about it... but it became a side project... and we have like *800* side projects now... so go, run with it! My thing is bad English. It, like, *kills* me. There is a *big* difference between writing something in German and putting it into Google Translate. Can't you just *pay* someone *ten dollars* to write me a paragraph? If you create a phrase and it's not exact, it's just one statement to get right, but it's important. Something that needs to be accepted here is that everyone speaks English and there is a certain level that has to be... that has to be... accepted! That's it... that's one of my big things... I can't, I can't, can't...

you can't take someone *seriously* if they don't know how to *check* something before sending it. I mean, if you have a website up? That text on your website? Should be… correct. I'm not saying perfect but… yeah, I agree, I'm not saying perfect but… I go to museums here all the time and their text is terrible… I mean their translation text is terrible! In a museum? That is embarrassing…

Yeah, that is embarrassing…

Yeah…

Yeah.

Yeah, well, I think this is going to work. We really like where you guys are at. You're, like… normal.

Yeah, we're not hipsters.

(They all laugh.)

We're not naïve and we're not pushovers, but we're not bad people, you know? …Well, thanks, guys. This is going to be great!

BRUNCH DATE

Here I sit across a cosy canal side café,
summer sun blazing.
It could all be construed as somewhat romantic, only
we are talking about art and music and politics
and common friends
in a way that might just suggest
we may just be pretending
we didn't just sleep together.
Call it a kind of 'urban ritual'
and, sure, it's better than you or me disappearing right 'after'
and I've played this charade before, you know.
I know all my lines;
I can exude casualness effortlessly.
But somewhere between your requests for a light,
queries of whether I take milk and/or sugar in my coffee,
I kind of want to cut our conversation short
and just scream

'WE FUCKKKKKKED'

just so I know it's real,
just so I know I didn't make it up.

AT LEAST IT'S NOT SUNRISE

Last Friday at Watergate, a club I swore would never go back to, on a night I swore I wouldn't go out. I'm taking chemical cocktails that keep me up until the sun forces my sunglasses on, and everyone around me is losing it. The DJ hands me a jug of Jäger; the promoter is cutting up lines and his eyes have that glint that suggests he's ready to seduce the boys who may not be that straight after they knock back the vial, the vial of the thing, the thing that some take to party and others use as a date rape drug.

One boy called himself the G-sexual. Sexuality defined by the substance he loved to take. And I can hear accents cut through bass lines. Tourists from London keep arriving. And at the end of the night I see a girl who has overdosed on this very drug that my party friends are on. A drug that I'd never even heard about until that Friday. And I'm amazed how everyone around me gets it together to take care of her, to shake her out of this daze. It should be a lot scarier than it is but it's too unreal to be scary. I feel like I'm in a film. I can see the skyline in the distance. I've missed the sun rising, now it's just day… but that was Friday, and now it's Tuesday. I was going to stay in but then I thought I'd check out this jam session until I ran into a friend who was having drinks in the back of Baghdad, where I enter the world's smallest smoking room.

Anyways, I'm doing my best to comprehend as much as I can of this group conversation in German, when this drunk skater boy with an open shirt rocks up, something retro Californian about him, or seventies porn star; I don't know, maybe it's the moustache? But I'm more distracted by this super-hot tiny Asian chick with him, wearing the greenest shortest dress imaginable, and then around the table I hear that skater boy had a birthday barbecue earlier in Görlitzer Park, only for some reason someone broke out pepper spray.

I can't process this, so I ask are we gonna go to the jam session? No one answers. Skater boy is wearing a flashing light necklace, it reads Hot… he takes us all to his flat around the corner. By now there are like fifteen of us and as we walk out I see this Irish boy I met at Bar 25 or kept meeting at Bar 25 every time I went

there this summer, my running joke with him being that he never ever left. So I say to him, 'Congratulations, mate, they closed, you're free.'

And he says he's so glad it's over, and I can tell he wants to find out where I'm going. It looks like a party in the making, but I don't really know him, so I don't invite him and feel like he must have this impression I'm part of this massive crew, when actually I only know three people there.

So we get to skater boy's flat, it's on the fourth floor. Flatmate is friendly but maybe not thrilled to have all of us randoms arrive, but it's early and we're not that drunk, and there are already twenty people there. But their vibe is more after-dinner party and our vibe is more party and then skater boy puts on that track 'Kühle Fliege' and cranks the volume right up.

People start ashing on the floor. I listen to the beat and the repeating vocal, and think about how here, here in Berlin, tracks that talk about being awake until morning, tracks about daylight coming, are always going to become anthems, they make you celebrate your party endurance, they make you celebrate the smiles you share with those you've never exchanged names or hellos with but kept running into Thursday, Friday, Sunday, weekend after weekend, dance floor to dance floor, this the city where partying past sunrise isn't hardcore, it's just normal.

But the party we're at now is not really a party. Flatmate turns down the music. So we all leave. And we get stuck on the corner by Baghdad again, and I'm kind of wishing I'd left with that Irish kid. He had said he was going to Club de Visionaire, where I could have seen my good friend Tony. But now I'm just on a corner with people I mostly don't know, getting quickly irritated by group dynamics where everyone is always responsible for at least one person, so when you try to leave someone says, 'Wait, I just need to get who just needs to get who just needs to get who just needs to get,' until you're a group again.

So we go to the jam but it's too early and there's a terrible band. Self-absorbed musicians with no soul, and an audience of onlookers who look too polite to walk out and seem scared of the stage. All standing as far back as possible.

We… are now only four. I guess we lost the others along the way. We don't stay long before we leave but I don't go home because I run into another friend, who I pluck from the sidewalk bar he's at, and wander with him somewhat aimlessly trying to agree on the best bar to have a nightcap in but everywhere's too empty, too boring, too Tuesday?

We end up in a bar on Falckensteinstr that was once a Kneipe, but is now frequented by hipsters. And we commiserate, about love and sex and relationships and closure, and I drink my double whiskey far, far too quickly. So we walk out, go through pitch-dark Görlitzer Park, until he must go one way and I must go another. By now my love advice has degraded to that of a thirteen-year-old boy. I drive off saying only, 'Ultimately we're all rubbish [meaning women], but then you all are too [meaning men].' And with those wise words I drive home, feeling civilised because at least it's not sunrise.

BIG THIS CITY MAY BE, BUT...

It's worth remembering you will run into the girl you suggested should leave her boyfriend behind and come with you. You will be served again by the bartender who saw you making out with a random girl in a dark corner at the back just days after making out with a random guy in the same bar, in the same dark corner in the back (the bartender will not judge you). You will meet the girlfriend of the boy who was flirting with you and you will see that hipster who one night was so drunk he could barely form sentences and yet still tried to come on to you (but the next time you see him he will pretend the night never happened). And the DJ whose advances you rejected one night will barely acknowledge your presence the next night. Sometimes you will see several of these people in the *same* night, just when you thought you would never have to see any of them again...

NETWORK

In my first moments back, Berlin impresses.
It's much warmer than the November I remembered,
or maybe after four years, I finally learned how to layer.

I am winding my way away from her old Kiez,
from the house share I spent so many hours in.
I am thinking about how everyone I knew no longer lives there
when I come up to the Ecke of Hobrechtstr and see him, the
only German I ever had a glimmer of something with, a man I
slept with, once.

When we met it was summer, and he has a different gait with his
winter garb, an impressively heavy coat and expensive-looking
boots, but the same flat cap and dark glasses. He used to live in
Prenzlauer Berg but I remember him saying he wanted to move.
As he approaches he slows down a fraction. I don't make eye
contact, knowing my woollen coat, knitted hat and glasses must
disguise me somehow.

I know if I stopped and called his name he would pause,
recognise me, maybe even hug me and then, and then… and
then what? What could we say?

'Hey, uh… how's it been since those years when we…?'

It's funny, though, because I did think of him recently. Two days
ago it was his birthday. I only know this because we're Facebook
friends. I wished him happy birthday electronically
and he… 'liked' it.

But two days later, when we run into each other, we don't even
stop to say hello? Isn't that strange? Maybe not. I guess that's
the kind of friendship Facebook is for. I keep walking, pass a
new bakery, think about how there's always a new bakery every
time I return, and when finally I settle into my place, I turn on
my laptop.

The network with the strongest signal has his name…

COUP DE FOUDRE

A pretty dark-haired girl on her bike stops you at the corner, asks you very shyly, very politely, in German, if you know a street called… and you will tell her shyly, very politely, in German, that you don't know it, but you are also trying to find out where it is.

So you make the kind of small talk on the way that your second language allows you to make, and when you arrive you discover that she is Australian, and she discovers you're English-American, and both of you will find it hilarious that you were speaking German.

And then you walk in and meet the other performers and as you wait for things to begin you fall into conversation with someone, then you fall into conversation with someone else, it's relaxed, it's pleasant. You feel ladylike in four-inch heels, a black lace and chiffon cocktail dress. You take a sip of your glass of wine, light your cigarette and…

Who, who are you talking to? What, what are you talking about? You were talking about… what? Where? Iceland?!

Nod, pretend to follow along… who was that?

Maybe you are talking about Brazil? Or, no, it was about how you can't write a novel, don't have the stamina and…who was that? Where has he gone?

Yes, you love touring. You're really thrilled about going to Madrid next. He's back, he's sitting down.

Now you're taking to some girl about poetry, no, maybe you're talking about literature, don't you remember that you met her before? It was in the autumn, at that English bookstore, don't you remember? No… I mean, of course… yes.

He's sitting next to you. That one… him.

The first sentences he says float high into the air over your head.

'Are you performing? Are you performing tonight?'

You say… 'Yes.' He says, 'Well… be sure to be entertaining.'

And when you're onstage, you're still outraged by that comment. How could he be so patronising? Now you… you are a full-blown cabaret act, all flashing lights and fireworks. If you were a musical, there would be a chorus line waving jazz hands.

And he will have no idea that it is all because of him.

THE BOX

You have been waiting for something.

You are waiting for a box. Full of things, artifacts of your previous incarnation. Your past life with her.

When she packs your books, sometimes a card or a silly note falls from the pages. At first she looks at or reads these things, and then decides it is best not to, to place them back, unseen.

And it's not that she is sad now for what can never be, but maybe just a little sad about the end of what was. Because that's the heart of it; even when something feels so final, so past-tense, there is the memory of that time when it was filled with promise and hope.

Nevertheless, now she will pack your things into the box, fold and pack things neatly, all that you left behind with her. When she takes it to be sent, watches it carried away, maybe she feels some pang of sadness. The last physical remnants of you are gone now, forever. Maybe she keeps some small thing behind, a sketch? A photograph? A note?

When the box arrived I asked if you were OK, and told you to call me if you felt strange later. Maybe you wanted me to go with you, to pick it up?

You didn't understand all my emotional commotion about your box. They're just your things, things that were left behind. You're getting them back because they belong to you, that's all.

When you unpacked you found that jacket you liked, and those shoes you forgot about and, damn it, the tripod is broken but you can dry clean the jacket to wear this weekend, on your birthday.

And when I walked into your room and saw that empty cardboard shell on the floor, gaping open like a hungry mouth, I felt a little down. I'm not able to explain to you why.

POSTCARD

The morning I leave, I find it impossible to slip away. The minutes tick over and pass, drawing perilously close to when I should have already left.

Finally, I force myself up. All of my movements misdirected, overwhelmed by clumsiness. Bleary-eyed, my limbs too long, stumbling in your room. I am the bull in the china shop, I think.

But at least I have everything packed now, just need to get my phone from the wall. I go to unplug it, but misjudge the space in the back corner of your room, turning only to narrowly miss knocking a stack of papers off the window ledge. But even half asleep I have cat-like reflexes, so catch the pile just before the first layers slip to the floor.

As I shift the papers back into their disordered order, the corner of an image is poking out. I can't make out what it is and I don't know what makes me do it. I think it must be a postcard and I instinctively think it's best to leave it alone.

But I pull it out ever so slightly anyway and I see it's a photograph of you. This is the first photo I've ever seen that looks exactly like you. Like I know you now. It could have been taken last week, it could have been taken yesterday. You look beautiful.

But then you are not alone in the picture. There is a girl, I'm not able to look at her for long. I couldn't really tell you what she looked like. Fair skin, dark hair. Maybe she had wavy hair or curls? I can't tell you what her facial expression was.

I don't look long enough, but I instantly knew who she is. And I feel guilty for seeing it and awkward for seeing it. I gently push the photo back into its place in the pile.

And then I feel… I don't know exactly how I feel. I feel strange and confused and jealous? No, not jealous. This is a feeling I have no word for; all I know is it isn't pleasant. Why, why am I affected this way? By a relic from a life before me. When you and I are always telling war stories.

But I shouldn't still be here now. What would you say if you woke up and saw me here? Silently standing.

If I don't go now I could miss my flight. I look back at you, curled up in bed peacefully. I think of the picture. I look back out of your window and floating through my head is this one sentence:

You were happy then.

And all I can think about is ending. The ending of the life you lived with her before I was known. And you are always quick to point out the mortality of things. And I know you're right, that nothing lasts forever and...

I don't have time to think about all this now. What good is it? I have to leave. I go to you. I kiss your mouth and kiss you gently on your cheek. I whisper in your ear that I love you. Outside the air is brisk and it is beginning to get light. I close your door gently behind me. It's time to leave. It's time to leave.

ACCRA

CHANGE, REMEMBER?

Me and the other two thirds of my family
collapse against our luggage trolleys,
our tired eyes scanning a baggage carousel,
as I notice that all the signs here are hand-painted
and fight for my attention, making up visual traffic.

All of the faces on the billboards
have dark skin, slogans that make me laugh like
Join the network that actually works!
We step through humid air, peel off our winter coats.
No, my father says repeatedly, we don't need help.

We don't need help.
I follow his lead,
shrug off multiple hands
that go for my suitcase, my bag,
waiting taxi doors that open for us.
In the back of the cab
my mum is buzzing.

She's a different person
chatting excitedly about how the roads
are so much better.
Do I remember?
Have I noticed, can I see
how much is changed?

It is familiar here, in a way.
But the bits I don't remember
could be change or they could just be
the bits I don't remember.
Mum keeps saying, 'But it's changed, aren't you impressed?'

My face registers nothing more
than bewilderment and she says,
'You don't remember.'
'You don't remember.'
'You don't remember, do you?'

OXFORD STREET

I told mum I wanted to go to Oxford Street.

They renamed it after the one in London because people say whatever you can find on that Oxford Street you can find here in Accra. So hours later we go.

The first words I hear walking down the street?

'Sister, sister, sister, come here, come!'

'Come look at my paintings/carvings/handbags/watches/ shoes. Maybe you want to buy my paintbrushes.'

My mum is proud of me getting all this attention and I am suspended in this constant state of introduction.

'This is my daughter. This is my daughter. This is my daughter, yes, my daughter.'

'Ahhh, your daughter. Maybe she won't go back. Sister!'

'Maybe you won't go back. Maybe you'll meet someone here, stay, you should stay here. Sister, I'm an artist, come, come look at my paintings/sandals/luxury watches. Let me show you – let me get you – do you like? Do you want to buy? Do you want one to take back? Don't you like it? Madam! Madam!'

I think to myself of a friend from Paris; she once said she gets really offended if she's called *Madam* rather than *Mademoiselle*, as it makes her feel old, miserable.

'Madam!'

I tell Mum that I want to walk back to the car and she's disappointed. I feel pathetic but I just don't want to be sold to anymore.

Please just let me find my way. Please just leave me at the hotel to sunbathe. Please let me get darker and maybe I'll stand out a little bit less.

EXCHANGE RATE

At lunch my father invited James, our driver, to eat with us. I could tell James did not want to. He would have rather waited for us by the car. By waiting he was taking a break. Coming with us, making conversation, just sitting with us meant he was still working. I did not know how to explain this to my father.

When we sat at the table to eat, I noticed James struggled with the cutlery, not knowing how to hold the knife and fork in his hands, hands used to dipping doughy balls of kenke into spicy stews of fish and goat.

When the bill came, 100 cedis for the four of us (€45.50), James was shocked. I'm sure he thought it was not just excessive but wasteful to spend such money on food. Even my father was embarrassed by the figure. He paid quickly and said it was expensive for him as well.

I met a poet in Accra who said, 'There are people in this country who live on 5 cedis (€2.40) a week. There are people who sell on the street all day, carrying their wares on their head.'

A great weight that they balance on their head, standing in the heat, rushing through traffic to make a sale.

They do this all day to make a total of maybe 2 cedis to bring home to their families. And this is what others will spend by lunchtime without so much as a thought.

None of my family ever ride in the tro-tros, the lorries that cross town crammed with as many passengers as will cram in. My family have cars and drivers, or book taxis.

The fare to cross town in a tro-tro is 40 pesewas.

In a cab it's 8 cedis.

€4.

Just over £3.

I can't get over the exchange rate.

COMPLICATED

You asked me, 'Why is it heavy?'

I said, 'It's complicated.'

Because how could I explain the boys who surround at the gates of Elmina Castle, welcoming me with one breath, pestering me for money with another?

How could I tell of the slave dungeons I walked into? The cells where the women were kept, there was a trap door in the ceiling. When a woman was chosen from the cell she could be brought up through the trap door in the middle of the night, kept in the room above, in the bed above until 'the act'.

My mum kept saying, 'But the children, the children the slave-owners had with them, they were given an education, given Portuguese names, raised as one of their own.'

Their mothers also would not be sent back to that cell; perhaps they weren't treated as wives but they were treated better than slaves, they were of a different class. And I thought to myself, *Yes, but it was rape that got them there.*

How can I explain of the cannons pointing skyward to a Dutch fort looming above? African tribes never had any interest in gunpowder, didn't fight with guns until the Europeans came to trade. The Europeans were clever; once one tribe had guns all the other tribes needed them. Suddenly a useless material became a valued commodity.

How can I describe my grandparents' house, aged with beautiful decay, where two uncles and two cousins were born and where my grandmother died? Where an uncle as chief mediates village disputes?

How can I describe my cousin's leafy gated community? The twenty-four-hour security guards, high walls topped with broken glass or barbed wire. Maids and cooks and gardeners who rise early and are in bed as soon as night falls.

And all the women I pass by in the car when we leave the gates. All those women on the roadside, walking all day in the dead hot heat, babies strapped to their backs as they step through all that standstill traffic, trying to sell whatever they have to sell: soap, toothbrushes, sunglasses.

How do I explain the strange pain I feel at hearing dialects brush past my ears without the slightest sense of comprehension? This ever-present sense of not being even the slightest bit Ghanaian?

The women in some stores who stare at me. The women in other stores who jump to attention as soon as I walk through the door. The woman who changed the CD to samba when I walked in her shop, asked me if I understood the lyrics. The blank way she looked at me when I said I was not Brazilian but half-Ghanaian. How do I talk about this constant admission of being Ghanaian, and the way those words often hovered in the air, foreign even to myself as if I was making them up?

What could I say about these young gorgeous Ghanaian women with older, much older unattractive foreign men? How I felt when my cousin said the most beautiful girls you'd see in those couples were often at the university, 'they had to pay their fees somehow'?

What would I say about the men who push by me, grab my arm to come back and talk to them, the eyes I can't meet if I don't want advances? And what about the women whose eyes I wouldn't dare meet with my own, scared if I let them linger too long what they (my eyes) might say?

This profound sense of wanting to fit, marred by the sense I never can, I never will.

No, I don't speak any of my mother's dialects. No, I can't remember what tribe my grandparents originate from.

No, I don't have any Ghanaian friends. No, I don't like bargaining, not at the market, on the street, anywhere.

Yes, I may have issues around personal space. Yes, they may not make sense here. No, I never quite feel relaxed here.

No, I don't want to take any pictures of... I don't want to take any pictures of... I do not belong here. I do not belong here.

And what am I left with, what am I at times suffocated by?

My hopes and impossible cultural aspirations, the desire to integrate, to intersect, and mostly, the failing and failing and failing.

DEPARTURE LOUNGE

WARNING

You should be very, very careful with what you tell me, you know.

It's not that I don't keep secrets. Secrets I'm fine with. No, what I mean is you should be careful with what you tell me. Even those things, especially those things you wouldn't even consider particularly private or interesting.

Because I will take them, I am saving them, preparing for when I will write about you. Because I could write about you at any time. The more time you spend with me, the greater the chances of it happening, the greater amount you give me to write.

It could happen after five minutes of speaking. Or it might not happen until five months later when you least expect it. By then maybe you don't even think much about the fact that I write. But I made a decision to write about you as soon as we met.

I'll expose you in some way. But don't worry; I will do it with consideration. I won't use your name or any specific physical description, but you will know it's about you.

You may not like it.

FALLING

I feel it happening again, and it is the most terrifying thing. This sense of suddenly losing ground, grappling with the air. And the descent, the descent is so swift, it distorts time. I must remind myself, *Keep breathing.* Then comes that fleeting sense of euphoria, of freedom. I can do nothing but let it happen. I might as well replace the fear with joy. Joy is how it began, after all. Don't be afraid, I tell myself, just let it happen.

On Boxing Day, we drove to a place by the English Channel called Beachy Head. When we arrived and got out of the car the view was insanely picturesque. I thought of it being painted, a backdrop on a film set, too beautiful to be real.

I walked up as close as I could to the cliff's edge. I looked down. My heart raced. I looked again. I could only stand the view for a few seconds. What is it with me and these kinds of heights? Why is it that poised, looking miles downward, all I can think of is how easy it would be to fall?

Take one step further and fall. What would the sensation be like? What would I shout out? Would I make any sound? And the onlookers nearby, what would they do then? There would be nothing anyone could do to stop it, to help me. Once I fell all anyone could do is let it happen. The last thing I would feel would be the icy chill of the sea as I hit.

I back up, look away, walk back, until I'm further and further up a hill, ambushed by the stunning landscape, surrounded by beauty. Every angle is gorgeousness, 360 degrees of calm. Every way you turn, another postcard. He joins me. Faced by all this loveliness, all we can do is smile and laugh.

I say, 'It's ridiculous, isn't it?'

He's trying to take a picture on his iTouch. When I say *trying*, I mean he takes a picture, looks at the result, compares it to the view, sighs, shakes his head, and tries again.

'I can't capture it.'

'No, you probably can't. Try remembering.'

He ignores me. I look back to the cliff. The hills are also beautiful, but the cliff, the cliff is… breathtaking. I think again of falling. I feel myself poised to fall, ground disappearing from under me, slipping. The earth spills between my fingers. It is the most terrifying thing. When you start, you can't stop.

WHY YOU SHOULD NEVER DATE A KÜNSTLER

1. **Conceptual artists**
Their art is the ***only* true art** in our post-modern age. They will give you credit for respecting their work (because you must be truly visionary to get it).

But then they will also make you feel like your work is less meaningful, because it's more light, or more humorous, or, God forbid… *commercial!*

Yet they will become hugely successful, go to fabulous parties where they hang out with Peaches and fantasise about motherhood together. They will say that the parties are 'part of work'. They will stop inviting you… before leaving you for one of the fabulous people at the fabulous parties.

2. **Musicians**
They're in a relationship already… with their instrument. They will either be in so many bands that their time is insanely stretched… or they will be in **a band** that you will refer to as **the band**. And if you ever dare say,

> 'It's me or **the band**!'

the answer is more likely to be **the band** than you. The connection with **the band** makes you feel jealous, so… you go to as many gigs as you can, until you know the set as well as (if not better than) **the band**, who sometimes are so drunk they can just about remember their songs.

And then there will be touring. And there will be that one girl after that one gig. Or maybe a few girls after a few gigs. And after many girls, after many gigs, after many tours, your musician will **leave you** either for one of them or for… **the band**.

3. **Poets**
Oh, my dears, steer clear. They're dreamy or moody or intense or if you're really lucky… **all these things at once**. They feed on

the highs and lows of human emotion. But they will be ever so charming, in a delicious way that curls around your skin.

They are all alcoholics, worse than many musicians. Seriously. They will definitely drink **more** than you. But you love words and they make them sound so good, and that's so hot. And they will be fantastic in bed, so much so that you forget their flaws, thinking you can work around them. But those mood swings and their intensity and their jealousy will come back to haunt you between those multi-orgasmic sexual marathons.

Then one day your poet will receive a compliment from someone who has made the conscious decision to go to a spoken word event, who tells the poet that their work is *awesome*, that they've seen them a few times. The poet will take their number, maybe even… take it a bit further…

And then when they next see you they will say *they can't handle being in a relationship, it's draining, it's affecting their writing, they've stopped writing, they need to be on their own and focus.*

And then you will find that, yes, they can handle being in a relationship, but the girl they make that exception for will not. be. you.

So you've had enough!
You go on a date with an accountant. You go on a date with a brain surgeon. You go on a date with a social worker. But it's just not working. You're about to give up altogether until you meet… the web developer. Who's chilled out and totally into you, who may be able to make you a website! It's almost too good to be true.

But you miss having intense debates about Turner prize winners, and one night over dinner you wish that they'd suggest books for you to read for a change. You invite them to go to the Wolfgang Tillmans show at the Tate but they don't want to go, so you go on your own and sit afterwards by yourself in the café.

The person sitting next to you asks what you were writing in your notebook. You ask what they were drawing in theirs. But honestly, you didn't see it coming.

Before you know it it's the sixth time you're meeting. You stay out late night after night in some French wine bar, trading opinions on everything from Dadaism to Bauhaus architecture. You're both crazy about Baldwin and Bukowski but unsure about Laurie Anderson, and before you know it, you've left your web developer
for an illustrator...

And the affair barely lasts, but who cares because now you know you are doomed
to keep dating artists.

PARIS

RUNAWAY

All I wanted was space, a disconnected space, a space for myself. But the timing. The awful timing of things.

I wanted to come here by train. I'm always flying and wishing I came by train. When you travel by train you go from centre to centre. You feel the distance of the journey, the rumbling of the carriage over land and water. You arrive thinking, *Yes, it's about time I arrived.*

But an airplane is a curious thing. You travel out to an airport, a space itself that feels abstract. Not as much as her sudden absence feels abstract, but still distanced, unreal, strange. You go out to a place outside a city, full of people waiting only to rush at the last minute to board. And maybe there are problems with security, and you're rushing only to wait again until you board. And in the air in two hours or less you are thrust into the heavens thinking, remembering.

I walk down Rue de Belleville thinking every Chinatown is a bit like every other Chinatown. I walk side streets towards the Republique thinking Hollywood only ever shows the pretty parts of Paris, this American idealised dream of Paris.

It never shows the grimy bits and ghetto bits or the edge you feel from some of the men. The way some of the men strip you down with their eyes, not flirtatious, not at all, more like directly invasive. I tried to tell you but you didn't understand. You said, 'You must like that.'

I walk through the streets of the Marais listening to language lessons. I meant to set them to French but even my iPod is confused. French and then German and then English. They start mundane but as they go to conversation they grow existential in tone, in their delivery.

Tomorrow will be…? Is it usually? Will it be warmer tomorrow?

Will it? Will it?

We are not invincible, but I know I treat my body as if it is. I push it past its limits, and why? A silly theory of mine from teenage days: the worse you treat your body, the less it demands. The more it can take. But no, that's a lie. All it leads to is a loss of conversation with your body, a complete lack of clarity of how it functions, what it wants.

Until it suddenly breaks down, shouts out, says you can no longer speak or breathing is tricky, or pains or noises, or maybe you can't run, or maybe you have to lie down until it tells you otherwise, sometimes long after you'd like. It's drastic, but it's the only way to get my attention.

So many times I've said, how can I tell the difference between the flu, a throat infection, or maybe just a hangover, or maybe I've just smoked too much? Why do I do it to myself? Why?

Now when I walk down streets that more than anything makes me feel overwhelmed, in the way, unnecessary. I think of her body when I last saw her in that hospital, only the third time I've ever been in a hospital. I think of her body. I think of its lightness in my hands as I held her, helped her to stand up, to walk to the restroom. The standing with her in the cubicle. The difficulty for her to even… even…

Standing there, trying to be normal about it. Somehow I was, because being with her I forgot myself. She was more important. I waited for her to tell me when she was ready for me to walk her back again. At least there was something now I could do for her.

Somehow she got a little strength when back in bed. She was telling us about boys in school and skipping school. Getting drunk at sixteen. Caught with some boy on some go-kart thing. She got expelled. 'Even then,' I said. 'You were that kind of girl even then.' And the three of us smiled.

Before she went to bed she told us that physical contact was good for her, so we each took a foot in hand and massaged. And I teased her, said, 'Oh, lady, I always wanted to get you in bed but not like this.' He played along: 'Ahhh, now she admits it.' She was disoriented but happy, face questioning, eyes like a child's. 'What? You're joking, right?' and I said, 'Oh, darling, I guess you'll never know.'

She laughed. And it was a beautiful sound, but not at all like her usual throaty laugh. It was a new laugh with the same lightness as her new frame; musical, glassy, like hanging chimes.

I kissed both of her cheeks, and maybe her mouth, I can't remember, but she hugged me after. We had to do it gently as she was so frail. We watched her fall asleep. She'd used up all her energy for the evening. We would be the last visitors that night. In my head I planned to see her again. I had no idea it would be the last time.

But any memory or eulogy doesn't seem right now. I find myself in a new place. I know there were reasons to come here but I lost them on the way. Tomorrow I think I want to spend all day getting lost; understanding, or maybe allowing myself to not understand it at all…

HEARTBEAT

I am no one here; I have no history. I don't need a name.

The language confuses, creates more distance, takes me away.

What is this place I'm in now? Who is it? I wonder, if a city is a person, what does it wear? How does it walk? If a city is a person, how do I know them? How familiar are we? Do we sit together, walk together? Do I feel attracted or repelled? Opinion can change with time, but really I know in those first minutes. What is the sound of its footsteps?

What is the sound of its heartbeat?

I think of sleeping with you, only sleeping. How do we sleep? I think of lying on my side, your arm, your body curled around me. Or maybe I rest my head on your chest, feeling the rise and fall of your breath, listening to your heartbeat. Sometimes my breathing follows your pattern naturally; sometimes I allow myself to sense the tempo. But sometimes I can't. Sometimes I can't even sleep.

Arriving here was like swimming upstream. I can't keep up. I don't belong. I don't have anywhere to go particularly, any reason to rush.

Those that live here, they have plans and schedules. They are moving to schedule, along paths and routes familiar to them. They do it without thinking, they do it automatically. They don't think of looking up at the buildings, of studying the shade of blue of the sky.

I am also like this in my city. Although Berlin is a funny kind of city, because in my Kiez, even those who live there seem to breeze around, reject the frenetic insistence of pacing, a sense of it all being pressing. I have more time. I take my time.

MAPS, TRANSLATIONS

Every day here I go out for a walk. Walk for the sake of walking. Every day I pace myself a little differently, slip closer into a collective rhythm. Play with this idea, even as an outsider, of walking in sync.

I'm OK with maps, but my sense of direction is terrible. I can remember places. But when I walk out of a store I've just walked into, my impulse is always to turn the wrong way. It's like maths; my brain jumbles, I panic, I need to really stop and pause and concentrate.

But I'm not scared of getting lost. I trust in the fact that even with a confused sense of direction I tend to find my way. The scenic route may take longer but it's often far more interesting.

I told him last night I wanted to get a map. Preferably the Paris equivalent of a London A-Z, so I could spend today getting lost. He laughed and said, 'It's not getting lost if you have a map to find out where you are.'

I thought about this as I went to sleep, and when I woke I thought about walking and running into myself.

I set out between four and five. I walk for hours and hours. I feel resolute in not taking along a map. I will find my way somehow. I feel convinced of that.

I have set myself a mission to get lost, to wander. To allow myself to be aimless. It's OK here, this is the only reason I'm here. I don't have to be anywhere, there is no one who will call me, there is no one to see.

I don't want to see anything specifically. I just want to walk, walk and feel like an outsider, enjoy it, all the foreignness.

I am getting used to certain things; to the awkwardness of my nonexistent French. And people see and hear me struggle but don't groan, are more patient than I expect.

The second day in the tabac the man corrects me, but not only does he correct me, he smiles after. Like the cab driver nights before whose amused 'bonsoir' greeted my overwhelmed 'bonjour' at 10pm. He seems to be saying, 'It's OK, but get it right.'

I follow impulses to walk down various streets and am annoyed by the smoking ban here. Don't understand Paris with a smoking ban. Consider bars and cafés and decide not to sit in any of them. And it's all OK; all of it is OK. Whatever I do by myself is OK. I only have myself to answer to. As I walk my thoughts race and rise in volume. I wish I could upload the thoughts directly to my laptop. Walking is another kind of writing. When I'm walking I am always writing. I walk and I think about travelling and tourism.

I want to discover something different. I am cautious about anything not French, any menu or sign in English, or, worse yet, menus with pictures and numbers. I try to steer away from anywhere I hear much English spoken. I try to search out the authentic.

I find one bar with a smoking area. Opulent velvet red and crystal chandeliers and art deco signage and it looks like the dream of what I want my French café to be until I walk up closer and yes, the sign is in English, but then I'm by the Place de Republique. I should know better.

Authentic. Authentic is the area I stay in. So many streets far from the idea of postcard pretty Paris. It reminds me more of parts of London I've lived in and loved. North African restaurants and Chinese places, as many places to buy noodles and couscous as baguettes and brioche. But it feels grim.

I want something… sparkly, shinier. You find yourself caring less about authentic. I am here partly for the ideal, the dream. And part of me, loyal to my own city, even says the grimy bits of Berlin may be dirty, but they're so much more charming than this… or are they?

I advise anyone walking around a city on their own to make a language learning lesson your soundtrack. It's both calming and strange. I am reminding myself of French, a language I tried to learn and completely forgot.

I am amused again by that pesky word *friend*, the translation of friend. In French it appears to have the same problem as German. Mon ami, my boyfriend… mein Freund, my boyfriend. No difference between boyfriend and boy friend. Suits the French really, I'm sure they like their ambiguity, but the Germans?

I always hate it when I'm seeing someone and they introduce me as a friend. I always feel awkward introducing someone as a friend who is much more than that. But it's that in-between stage, it's tricky…

What do you say? 'This is [insert name]' is probably best.

'Une bouteille de vin blanc' helpfully plays just as I linger outside a wine shop. I take it as a cue, but buy a bottle of red instead. And then walking out (which way am I headed?), small talk, polite conversion. My least favourite questions. For example: what do you do?

Possible answers given.

I am in education, I am in finance. I am an architect. I am a writer.

Naruna calls me on Skype that night. She has her gleam back, is full of brilliant non-sequiturs, says no one has a relationship with an artist. Artists have relationships with themselves and occasionally let you in for a threesome. And I think she's right.

In my temporary home. Drinking wine and stuffing my face full of macaroons, I relax in her kitchen. I think about cities. My relationship with them. I treat them like people, and like people I'm not always good with first impressions. Sometimes those I resist are the ones I should spend more time with. Put more work into, as he likes to say. I hear this one saying:

'I don't need you, but there is something for you here. Find it, and take it with you. If not, I will be here when you come back again.'

OU EST LES HIPSTERS?

We catch up outside a very cute bar near Gare de l'Est, huddling outside under a heater (because I've yet to cope with the reality of the smoking ban). After five or ten minutes of talking an ancient-looking man sitting alone beside us requests we talk quieter. I am bent on finding the solution to the question my travels have failed to answer thus far.

Ou est les hipsters? Ah, there they are.

In bar/club/bistro La Fidélité.

Upstairs in the restaurant, which is gorgeous and appears to have great food, is some kind of private party with a black and white dress code. Fitting, really, as colour isn't something fashion dabbles with easily here.

This, the city synonymous with chic, where they have mastered the art of artfully posing and created the perfect soundtrack to pose to. Electronic, chilled, not too beat-heavy, the odd nineties hip-hop/pop track thrown in for ironic good measure. Is it cruisey? I'm not sure. A lot of people talking, not really dancing, but then strictly speaking I suppose it isn't a club.

I'm reminded of Stockholm. Initially the fact that you are in a room where everyone has a perfect body and perfect bone structure and dresses like they have walked off a fashion shoot (not edgy enough for *Vice* or *i-D*, but maybe *Vogue* or another magazine) is overwhelming. But it stops being intimidating when you realise, perfect or not (my mate calls this crowd average by Paris standards), everyone starts to look a little the same.

Toilet queues are generally a good place for the style and posing gauge, and at this place they don't disappoint. I subtly survey the line-up of ladies and gents in front of me (it's unisex here, you see). The ladies are a little black dress brigade in four- to six-inch heels, bags and belts in this season's camel and leopard, perfectly applied red lips (all in a nearly matching shade). They are girly, sleek, porcelain-skinned, doe-eyed, but… dare I say it, in their similarity, not that striking.

When I descend down the stairs only one woman in the vast restaurant catches my eye. She is the only girl in the place who dares to wear red, a floaty loose scarlet maxi dress, belted with some gold cord.

I learn my first Paris style lesson: it's easy to stand out in the crowd, all you need is a bold dash of colour.

She stands like the beacon of style she must feel like, and she does look amazing in the sea of black and white attire. I watch her walk down the stairs to the club and follow her at a cautious distance.

The crowd in the bar/club/smoking area is also ridiculously good-looking. It appears every single man has perfected smart casual, urban smart, but loose with it. All have beards, dark hair, one out of four has glasses. The girls with cropped pixie cuts, or shampoo-commercial shiny long tresses. They have painted on skinny jeans and blouses, or, more likely, short stunning dresses, well cut, fit to form. The ratio of men to women is definitely in a lady's favour. But wait, I've lost the girl in the red dress. How did that happen? The room is so small.

Of course, there she is. DJing. That's where her style bravery stems from, then.

Drinks are served in plastic cups and are ludicrously expensive. Apparently the place shuts at one, even at weekends, which usually would be an hour I arrive somewhere. But tonight, despite the lovely company of my friend, I kind of want to go home. One more drink, she says.

I don't feel like another long drink, and I've had so much wine in the last days I feel like it's coming out my pores, so I suggest a shot. I don't realise they don't really do that here. She goes to the bar, returns with two tiny plastic shots of vodka, tells me a minor stir was caused at seeing and hearing her order them. But the real punchline was the cost: €5 for a shot? Gosh, we are spoiled in Berlin.

I walk home. No more or less impressed with Paris nightlife than any previous trip here. I get a little lost and take longer to find my way home. And as I walk down the streets and try to remember where I'm going, the snow falling under the street lights is silly gorgeous.

It's almost unreal. It looks less like snow and more like silvery confetti. It doesn't stick to the ground, or my coat. It makes me think, even the snow here is high-heel friendly. How terribly appropriate.

LONDON

NOT EVEN WORTH STEALING

In the insurrection
when teenagers took to the streets
stealing sportswear,
hijacking HD TVs,
cornering corner shops as they
filled their pockets with packages of cigarettes
and wine coolers

before the revolution was televised
news of it spread swiftly
through BlackBerry Messenger
long before those convicted
would be imprisoned
for stealing bottles of water.

In the insurrection
when teenagers took the streets and took over,
when the H&M towers toppled
and thousands of pounds'
worth of high street fashions
were rapidly ripped down from their rails,
amongst the mass of stolen
jeans and jewellery and perfume
and laptops and flat-screen TVs

in the abyss
of shattered glass and ash and smoke,
every bookstore was...
untouched.

If rioting is the voice of the unheard
I hear this message clearly.

In that moment when
you're in mob mentality,
long before later
(when you may think better of what you've done),

in that moment
when you can take,

when no one can stop you,
when you deserve to take yours,
when the bankers have been taking theirs, haven't they?
and everyone's in on it, aren't they?
and the group is goading you on
to take, take, take,
when you think,
I can take anything.
What do I want?

ranked up alongside
the sportswear and electronics a book
isn't worth so much.
This isn't a revolution;
this is consumerist warfare.

What am I talking about?
Why am I even questioning?
Who would ever steal…
a book?

A book!
It's just some paper, some ink.
Some words, some stories, some images,
some heart some sweat some nerves.

What is a book worth, anyway?
You can't quickly sell it
from the back of a car.
What's a book when compared to
a tracksuit, an iPad, a laptop?

In the insurrection, when teenagers took to the streets,
taking anything and everything they wanted,
not a single book was stolen.
Every bookstore remained
untouched…

COMMODITY

I couldn't believe my luck when he walked in.
I know it's embarrassing
but I've got this weakness
for hipsters,
particularly the extra-tall, extra-skinny,
skinny jeans and
glasses-wearing kind.
But all that aside, he was cute, charming,
and it was alarming
how our favourite bands, films and fine artists agreed,

our cultural interests slyly winking
as if to say,
'The deal is done.'
His forties army coat and braces
flirting with my vintage fox fur and heels.

So after two or three or five more drinks
we sauntered over to the pub that
Vice magazine owns
and watched some unsigned band
we were both sure we had heard of.

And then I feel his fingerless glove
against my neck
and we're kissing
and it's wicked until we break apart
and he says (in his cute Kent accent)
that he had been so excited about our date because I was this

hot BLACK chick.

And it's not that it wasn't a compliment, exactly.
Maybe what bothered me
is the word he emphasised most was *Black*.
And I think he got it
because he quickly added that
that made me something of a 'commodity' on our scene.
And until that moment
I hadn't actually noticed.

Until that moment
it didn't really matter.

But now, the label 'commodity'
hung somewhere between
my bootleg Chanel
and American Apparel and
sure enough, I was the only Black girl
in a room of, like, sixty.

'You see?' he said, and I nodded
and I wished we hadn't stopped kissing
or maybe that
we hadn't left the last bar.

Or maybe at least if I was being worn like
some kind of badge of chic cultural diversity
that he could have kept it to himself
so I could have left feeling that
I was hot, not a commodity.

REAL

I used to love going to strip clubs. I used to spend the kind of money on strippers that would have sustained a cocaine addiction. I used to go to strip clubs a lot. What did I get off on? Are you serious? Everything!

Beautiful women with perfect sinewy legs.
Bodies in dimly lit casino kitsch spaces undulating to bass, trembling through thighs with hip-shaking beats.

But what I got off on was eye contact. I loved the eye contact, it made it more **real**.

The thing about a table dance: a table dance is intimate, not as intimate as a lap dance but intimate enough. If you've never had one, let me explain: you sit in a chair, legs spread as wide as you can, and then the stripper, she dances between your legs, bends over, *gets right up in your face*, and you can't touch, and the tension, well… that's part of the fun.

But what I got off on…was eye contact. I wanted to cement the fact that this was not just one of a million acts she was performing. No, I wanted to make it clear that I wanted this, she was doing it for me… and twenty seconds later, I'd see a change in her eyes, a hint of a smile, something in her understanding that I wanted her only. I wanted her specifically. Well… for the moment, anyway.

It must have made it better than all the horrible men she had to dance for. She would understand I wanted her on a deeper level… it made the interaction more **real**, I thought.

There was one club I went to that was women only on Tuesdays. I was such a regular that when I went on my birthday, all of the dancers wanted me up on stage. There was one in particular who was flirting with me intensely… but she must be like that with everyone; I didn't take her seriously. I never expected to see her out of that club.

I'm not sure how long after that night it was. It might have been a year or maybe only several months. I was sat in a caff in my neighbourhood, ready to sink into whatever tabloid newspaper had been left behind, when a voice called out my name. But the woman who had called it out wasn't someone I had ever met. I thought she must mean someone else; my name is pretty common. But she called it out again and this time gave me a little wave. She crossed the café, sat across from me. I still had no idea who she was. I remember thinking I had never been so close to someone wearing so much make-up.

'Live around here, then?'

she said.

'Yeah, sorry, I… where do we know each other from?'

She laughed. Told me a name, said it was her stage name, but she didn't mind me knowing her real name, which she told me as well.

She told me I looked good, it was nice to run into me. She was happy to have my company, launching into her affairs with overly personal detail until something in her features finally clicked. I hadn't recognised her because she wasn't looking so great. Her foundation was caked, eyeliner winged at angles I couldn't work out. The grey hoodie and faded jeans hung off her emaciated frame, a far cry from the curves and glittery thong, and she was talking… a lot.

She was telling me about feeling lonely, not having many friends, getting bored with dancing but the money was so good, and if she wanted the free time and the cash, she couldn't do anything else, and her love life was a mess, but now running into me maybe that could change. She winked.

She spoke of her son having trouble at school, and his father not being much help, and through all of this, I found it really hard to hold her eye contact because she was no longer someone I could project my fantasies onto, she had become far too **real**.

I avoided the caff after that. Years later I went to a strip club with a girlfriend but it wasn't the same. I couldn't get off on it. I never went to one again.

BACK

This is my city. These are my neighbourhoods.

Here my heart beats in sync. Here I can pass through crowds with enviable ease. I'm not rushing here, but I like to keep up a pace.

For the days that I am back again I have a perfect sense of direction. It's instinctive. It's flawless. No one impedes my flow.

Trains arrive as I step onto platforms. Tourists carrying suitcases up stairs stop, smile and gesture for me to go by. Doors are held open for me as I enter and exit busy stores. Maybe I am meant to be here.

It is a big city, but it is a city of villages. So many people following the same grooves again and again in circles. Spinning and repeating themselves over and over like scratched records.

In the tube I accept that the speed and length of the journey is out of my hands. I occupy myself by writing, reading, people-watching. I like people-watching. I especially like making eye contact.

It's not quite the done thing here. It amuses me how most don't even acknowledge the gaze. A few return it with shyness, blushing maybe, or, worse, return aggressive glares. So I give up the game.

This morning I noticed a gorgeous young man walking into Angel station. He had cheekbones you could cut something on. He wore this eccentric but chic ensemble of tweeds and tartan; something Viv Westwood about it, striking, set off by his massive afro. I have no idea who he is. But I saw him this morning at Angel, and I just saw him an hour ago again this evening, walking out of Marble Arch.

It is a large city, yes, but it is also just a series of connected parts.

I USED TO FANCY YOU

She's just as attractive as I remember, if not more. The look she gives me when I greet her makes it abundantly clear she has no idea who I am. But in any case, if I'm unknown to her, she seems more than happy to make my acquaintance.

I want to play along, but can't control my amusement.

'Lady... hey... it's me, remember...?'

Her eyes, shifting and focusing, locking into place as if working out a complex equation, and then... she throws her arms around me. I think we may even end up holding hands.

'Oh my God, oh my God, oh my God, oh my God, it's you!'

The bar I'd been heading to is closed. I manage to signal to the friend I'm with that I've been kidnapped by this girl as he joins her friend and we all walk along. And now she is talking in a breathless ramble, zigzagging down the pavement, clinging to me. I try my best to help her maintain her balance.

She tells me how happy she is to see me, but that she's been very sad lately. She doesn't want to tell me why, but she is very sad and most of all, she is very, very drunk. I nod and smile and tell her again and again that it's OK, that I'm happy to see her as well. Funny to run into her, really, as I don't even live in the neighbourhood, or the city, or the country anymore. But then it's such a small world, isn't it?

She's very drunk, she says. Maybe we should pass on having another drink, I say. My friend seconds this; it's Thursday, we're both skint. We'd really be fine with turning the corner and walking home.

But: 'No, no, no, no, no,' the girl says. She hasn't seen me in ages, and she's not working tomorrow, and all she wants is one or two more drinks, and her other friends have left, so please could we not be so boring and walk five minutes with her to a very, very, very near pub?

So me, my friend and this girl's friend walk along. It's a much longer walk than the promised five minutes. She gets my attention again. Makes sure we're walking a little further ahead, needs to make sure no one else is listening. It's very important I listen. It's very important I hear what she has to tell me. There's something she's always wanted to tell me, she can only tell me now, because she's very drunk.

'I really used to fancy you,' she says.

I say that's very sweet of her to say, and, feeling her struggle to walk straight, am about to suggest again that maybe we should skip this drink. I'm feeling more and more like we should meet another time. But 'no, no, no' we can go 'just for one, just for one' and did I hear her? Did I hear her say she used to really fancy me? And no, she isn't a lesbian. That would be fine, but she isn't. And actually I'm the only girl she's ever fancied, but it used to really mess with her head.

I'm not sure what to say or how to take this.

But it's OK because she'd worked out it wasn't a sexual thing. She just really liked me then and thought I was really cool and beautiful, but it's OK now.

It used to really mess with my head. It's cool, don't worry about it.

And I appreciate it's important for her to tell me this but now more than ever, as her monologue repeats, it starts to make me feel anxious.

We get to the bar; we just about get last orders. Afterwards she suggests that me and my friend go with her to another late-night bar. But we don't really have money, and it's not really walking distance. But she says please, and she's paying the cab fare, and she'll get our drinks, and she's so excited we're going with her. She's not working tomorrow. 'OK, OK, OK,' we say, and relent.

At the bar, after she gets a round, she disappears to the dance floor. I try to find her for a while, and then give up, going instead to the smoking courtyard. I get talking to a boy I think is my friend Florian from Berlin, only to discover it is really my friend Naruna's friend Etienne from Paris. Then some lovely east London gay boy is talking to me about how everyone here is Spanish. 'Shhh, just listen,' he says.

So I listen and he's right and hey, what happened to that girl I came in with? I'm a little worried. Should I look for her? Should I be worried? 'No, of course not,' my new friend says. 'It's a nice local bar, a gay bar, nothing bad can happen, what bad thing could happen to a girl in a nice local gay bar? Relax. Smoke another cigarette.' He lights all of my cigarettes. I really like talking to him, this is turning out to be nice chilled evening and then a bouncer walks up to me and asks me to come out right now, something has happened to the girl I came in with.

When I walk out the front doors the first thing I see is the police cars, then the ambulance. I walk to a police car and peer through the back window to see my long-lost friend, her right eye puffed up and swollen as if she's been punched there. What happened? The police regard me with piercing glares. She was very drunk, how could I have left her by herself? She had walked out and hit her head on the pavement. If I could be at all helpful maybe I could convince her to get into the ambulance.

She insists everyone is making a big deal out of nothing. I somehow coax her into the ambulance. Sobered by the sight of her, too broke to even get the bus, I walk the thirty or forty minutes it takes to get home. Smoking the last of a ten-pack of cigarettes and all I can hear in my head is the echo of the ambulance sirens, and her saying again and again,

'I used to really fancy you, you know? You're the only girl I have ever fancied. And it really used to mess with my head.'

DEAR STRAIGHT GIRL

Wait, let me specify,
because I wouldn't want to generalise unfairly.
Dear straight girl that I met
at the Gaiser party
Sunday night at Fabric
on the first of March –
well, technically the second –
sometime between 3am and 4.

What happened?
Did you suddenly come down from
the drugs you had taken?
Or just feel differently
with your friends at your side?
OK. Rewind.

Before you'd entered my thoughts
I was just hanging out in the DJ box
watching over the dance floor,
this sea of fist pumping,
camera flashing, light strobing,
minimal techno mayhem.

I was hanging out with my mates, the DJs
Jacob and Cormac and Peter and his girl Sonoya.
I didn't know you were out there yet.
I couldn't care less that you existed.
I was in the middle of this
exclusive private party
elevated above the masses.

Dear straight girl,
later I left the DJ box,
lost myself in this ocean of ravers
when that bass line dropped
and with that bump of K
and the dab of MDMA
and the Jäger and the whiskey
and the Red Bull coursing through my veins.

My eyes clocked you, first once
then twice
until, caught up in that eye contact game,
my eyes dilated and took in all six feet
of that page three girl frame
in glorious chemically enhanced technicolour.

Dear straight girl,
you're not even my type!
OK… well, you're kind of the kind of girl
that's anyone's type,
what with the legs that never ended
embraced in black spandex
and the corseted C-cup breasts
barely covered up by your
'ironic' rock band top.
Yes, you caught my attention
but I feel I must mention
that you kissed me first!
You told me that I was 'hot'
and I… I… well…
I was too mashed
to articulate much

but I did manage to tell you
that you looked really good
against the wall I had you pinned to.
But I was fine with just dancing.
It was you! you! you!
who guided my hands
to an access-all-areas pass
to go wherever they wanted
(which was everywhere).

Dear straight girl,
you were far from complaining.
Dear straight girl,
you were definitely reciprocating.
Dear straight girl,
when you put your hands up my dress

I immediately decided to break
my new law abolishing
one-night stands and toilet cubicle sex.
I was ready to make allowances
for you!

Dear straight girl,
what happened?
Your friends appeared
and then there was this transition.
Someone said something about leaving.
You were swiftly agreeing.
Suddenly you couldn't leave fast enough.

Dear straight girl,
I wish I didn't remember your name.
Dear straight girl,
I'm sure
you didn't commit mine to your memory.
Dear straight girl,
I hate the way you left,

instantly transforming me from
this fabulous hedonist
at this exclusive private party
to a girl on her own
in a raver ocean
not nearly close enough to home.

Dear straight girl,
you know what?
This has all been irrelevant
because we'll probably never meet again
and you will never
hear this poem.

CLARIFICATION

The girl I briefly dated who said,
'It's just that I want to have kids.
I mean, I know I'm only like twenty but
I'm already thinking about them
and I am attracted to women
but what if we got serious
and we wanted to have kids and—'

I… am not that.

The girls who throw themselves
at each other in the bar
so their boyfriends can watch
or make out madly in the middle of the club
to drive all the men around them
mad with lust –

nooooooooooooooooooooo.
I. Am. Not. That.

But I am no less attracted to men
because I've had relationships with women
and I am no less attracted to women
because I love leggings and high heels
and I am just as likely
to arrive at your dinner party
with a girlfriend or a boyfriend.

But my life is not
this rich pageant of threesomes
and free sex
although sometimes I wish
that rumour was true.

I knocked down a walk-in closet
full of dresses to come out
to my mother and my boyfriend
before I was of a legal age
to vote, or drink.

Back in the days
when I first hit the gay scene
I quickly worked out a few things.
Like very few women wanted women
who also dated men.
It was already suspicious
if you were feminine.
And I wanted in.

So I ditched *bisexual* for *lesbian*.
Shaved my head.
Threw all my dresses in the closet.
Carefully tucked behind them
any passing interest in boys I came across.

And I believe that sexual identity
is not a decision
but it is worth mentioning
it exists on a continuum.
So after close to ten years
of being a card-carrying member
of the lesbian tribe
I. Met. This. Guy.

And the thing about repression
is if you dam the waters long enough,
when they break
get ready for floods.
I remember vividly
one summer morning
walking down grey London streets

when it seemed as if every bus stop had
some gorgeous tall
broad-shouldered guy,
baggy jeans, low-rise,
lazy arrogant swagger,
or some fantastically foxy curvy female,
legs elongated by skyscraper-high heels,
hips swaying to a rhythm in my head.

By the time I got to work I panicked,
because if this was what it was like
to go for both genders
how was I ever gonna get any work done again?
And if you think it must be great
to have both genders at your disposal,
it must make the opportunities for dating exponential,
let the record serve:
when it comes to my scorecard
my track record consists mainly of
going for guys that are taken
or girls that are straight.

And, boys, believe:
the relationships I have with women
are definitely serious.
But gay girls take heed:
liking guys should not
make me a subject
of risk assessment.

And if you're thinking,
*She must prefer sex with the same
or opposite,*
stop…
let's just say
it's different.

But if you're interested,
boy or girl,
what I'm most interested in
is if we can connect,
because I am more than ready
for that.

SPACE ODYSSEY TO THE BUNKER
WITH NO BUZZER

The first time I stepped into the bunker with no buzzer
I thought
this might be the world's smallest room…
but he didn't have much
so there was more than enough
room to move in, but it seemed, no matter
how we passed one another,
it was impossible not to touch.
Not in a way that was intentional,
definitely always accidental, our arms and shoulders brushed.
Sized one another up, maybe even flirted with
the idea of more intimate contact;
this was a protected space,
scorpions' tails crossed at the gate,
and there we spent a full day, a full-on full day
and the evening aftermath:
I complained that the bars
in Hackney didn't stay open
late enough
and bought myself a flask of Jack Daniel's from the corner
shop
as consolation and when we came back
nothing really happened.
Well, there was a lot of talking about all sorts of things
but mainly relationships, and then I think we traded
notebooks,
teased one another over
the hieroglyphics we used masquerading as handwriting;
nothing happened
but that room felt
charged with something.
Months later I lingered outside that same
Graham Road grey door
waiting to enter,
stepped up the stairs,
and though it still may have been the world's smallest room
on this day it amazed
how we consistently

navigated the space
so no matter how we passed one another
there was definitely no chance of touching.
And I still felt protected by the scorpions at the gate
but maybe not quite as relaxed as the time before;
this time it felt like
there was just enough room for us and our alter egos,
perhaps some space left over
for the lives we were leading outside,
both more than a little preoccupied with the thoughts of.
And the hours didn't pass quite as fast
and when we finished I made no complaints
about bars not being open late enough;
I was long gone before closing times,
leaving me to run and catch buses and centre my mind on
the concept of space,
the space we occupy,
the space we choose to share,
the space I so often reveal to complete and total strangers
but sometimes struggle to explain to those that I intimately
know,
the space two flights up
from this unmarked
Graham Road grey door,
the bunker with no buzzer,
the safe haven for a poet
and the space he fills,
the space between our meetings,
the space underneath what is said
and what lies unspoken
guarded by scorpions'
tails crossed at the gate…

POCKET WARMER

Do you know,
have you ever seen
one of those
pocket warmers?
You get them in the winter
to keep you warm.
They fit…
in your palm…

He had a thing about hearts. Heart-shaped things. So I gave
him a box full of heart-shaped things for Valentine's Day, a
heart-shaped holiday. I spent a whole afternoon making that
box. Sat in a café writing literary quotes about hearts on the
back of postcards with images of hearts on the picture side.
There was silvery glittery confetti, confetti hearts all along the
side.

When I gave it to him, I watched him open it gingerly.
Revealing all these hearts I had assembled for him. He
seemed… mystified. Maybe my gesture was too much? I felt
embarrassed, silly, childish.

He said, 'Thank you,' sincerely enough. But he had to admit
that maybe I'd taken this heart thing too far. The one thing he
did like in the box was this pocket warmer… heart-shaped…
he was really excited about it. He liked to keep it with him, in
the cold. Do you know what a pocket warmer is? Have you
seen one before? You put it in your pocket when it's cold to
keep your hands warm. To keep you warm. The one I gave him
was heart-shaped.

Do you know how they work? OK, well, the first time is kind of
magical. There's this little metal disc inside. When you press
on it, it starts a reaction. A reaction that spreads through the
substance inside. It literally courses with energy. It stays warm
like this for hours, and then the substance hardens.
And it isn't warm anymore.

The next time we met, we pressed on that disc
but nothing happened.

Because the second time is less easy.
The second time takes work

You have to heat the thing,
slowly,
in a saucepan of boiling water for hours
until it's warm enough to take out into the cold. I didn't know
this when I gave it to him. I thought you could always press
on that little silver disc in the centre. I didn't know that kind of
magic only happened once.

Last night he came to see me. It was raining. I saw him arrive
through frosted glass. I had a gig that evening. I was talking to
the host. She was asking me about myself. About what I did.
What did I want people to know about me?

I am not a good person.

'Oh, um, say…

'I'm from a lot of places.'

I hurt people.

'I have an album coming out…'

I hurt people I love.

'It's free, you can download it for free.'

I hurt people who love me.

I go to him. He's wearing his favourite coat. It's silver. There's a
pocket over the chest. He puts my hand there. It's warm. I try
to pull my hand back, but he holds it there, opens the pocket,
hands me… this heart. This heart-shaped thing. The pocket
warmer.

He's looking at me. It's *heartbreaking*. I hate the word heartbreaking. How can a word so painful be so overused?

Heart… breaking…

He's asking me if I have any pockets. I panic.

'No, no, no, I don't. I'm – I'm wearing a dress. I'm wearing a dress. I don't have—'

'Your coat?' he says. I'm shaking my head.

'I-have-no-pockets,' I say (with my hands thrust firmly inside them).

I want to scream. Because I know what will happen. He will put it in my pocket and later it will cool. I will look at it crumpled in my hand into some horrible shape and think
this is my fault, he gave it to me and this is what I did.

It's all so silly. It's only a pocket warmer. But he made it symbolic, romantic. When romance becomes dirtier than a four-letter word like love.

When I find it again (in my bag now, long since moved from the pocket of my coat) I am outside a train station, smoking. Above me a flower bed hangs. A droplet of condensation, cold and wet, lands on my face, slides down my cheek, resembles how it feels. It's fitting because, as much as I want to, I am unable to cry.

Do you know… um… have you ever seen those pocket warmer things?
You get them in the winter to keep you warm.
They fit… in your palm.

ARRIVAL/DEPARTURE

As sliding doors opened, I stumbled in with my two bags and suitcase. I fought for a space to stand, as my eyes collided with his. I looked down, away. Stops later I turned, and caught him looking again. I had been lost in thought. I was wearing a black Chanel oversized T-shirt, oil-slick black leggings, gold hightops, a leather jacket covered in studs. I still had my massive sunglasses on. There may have been mascara stains just beneath them, the remains of tears.

When it was time to get off, I fought my way through the crush of rush-hour commuters. When I looked up ahead, I felt like Sisyphus at the mountain. Why oh why did this station have to have so many fucking stairs? Suddenly my train voyeur was there. Did I want help with my suitcase? My yes was all shades of grateful.

'Good holiday?' he asked. In my mental state of departure, the fact I could be arriving didn't gel. It's funny, that, isn't it? Someone coming or going: how can you ever tell? Whether we are coming or going, we look the same.

I'd paused too long; he was struggling with my suitcase, but still seemed intent on hearing an answer. I mumbled…

'Uh… kinda.'

'Kinda a holiday?' He smirked.

'I kind of live here part of the time, so it wasn't really a holiday. I'm on my way back to Berlin.' There was a level of exasperation in my voice. The statement sounded strange to my ears, more glamorous than the reality. What would I think if I met my doppelganger and heard such words? I'd probably want to ask what she did for a living, and look at the gold trainers and gold bag, and think about what the cities of London and Berlin had in common. I'd then decide she was either a DJ or an artist.

Maybe he thought all this, maybe he just accepted it; at any rate he nodded and in a considered way, as if putting pieces of a puzzle together, said, 'Which I guess is where you live the rest of the time.'

He told me he'd be going to Vienna soon. The mention of the city cheered me up for some reason.

'Oh, it's gorgeous, I've been twice this year.'

'Yeah... I'm from there. But I haven't been in ten years.' His accent was completely London. 'The thing is, I'm going because... I'm going to see my dad. We haven't seen each other in...well... we don't get on so well.'

I nodded. This was the preamble to a conversation that could be interesting or meaningful but would have to end prematurely. I saw the barriers to my line. We stopped. He needed to go the other direction. For a moment it was almost as if he was considering walking along with me. I quickly interrupted the pause.

'Good luck. It is an amazing city,' I said.

He handed me back my suitcase. 'Well...' He searched for something else to say. 'Have a safe journey.'

'You too,' I said.

I walked off, and as I reached the barriers I looked back to see him looking in my direction, before turning and walking away.

INVERNESS, MADRID, DRESDEN, MARBURG

THE GREAT ESCAPE

I was on a train to Inverness. Her bag was almost as big as she was and nearly twice as heavy. To get it down the aisle of the carriage she had to stand it on one end. Her whole self wrapped around it as she walked it along with slow deliberate steps. The carriage was shaky. It was tricky to keep moving the bag along, but she managed.

He might follow her. She wasn't sure if she cared if he did. He was turned away when she got up from the seat and left. He didn't watch her walk away as she struggled along with her bag. He was keeping himself to himself, trying to remain calm.

She made it through one carriage, and then the next, and then the next. She didn't know where she was going, only that she had to keep moving to get there. She found herself in the luggage compartment between carriages on the far side of the train. She propped her bag against the others. Across from her were an old man, a young mother and small child all waiting to use the bathroom. I was stood on the other side. I stared at her for a moment too long before looking away. She steadied her bag again.

What was she doing here? What was she doing? She found a little space for herself beside the window and pulled it all the way down. She pushed her head out above it as far as she could. She watched the landscape rush by. Lush valleys led to lakes and rolling hills. Even as it rained it was beautiful. She wanted it to calm her. She wanted…

He was there now, standing behind her. How long had he been there? She heard him say her name. His voice was unintelligible. It was as if someone had knocked a radio between two frequencies. She looked at him, saw his mouth moving but couldn't make out any words. She turned away. He placed a tentative hand on her shoulder. She bristled, shrugged it off. He, visibly wounded by this, stepped back, turned away. Softly he called out her name again. People around them were watching now. She knew he didn't like that.

She pushed her head forward out the window again. Greedily

sucked in gulps of rain-soaked air. She wanted to inhale the landscape. She was trying to breathe. She was finding it hard. He had gotten louder, he was standing behind her now. He was going on and on and she heard someone else ask when they would get to the next stop. The conductor saying, half an hour.

Outside it looked peaceful. Outside she could surround herself with sky and breeze and hills, all she wanted was...the train stopped... there was an announcement of flooding on the tracks ahead. They would be stuck there for an hour at least. Her boyfriend touched her on the shoulder again. He said, 'Come on...'

She nodded. Pulled open the latch of the door she was leaning on, jumped forward, door slamming shut behind her as she ran. Ran fast through fields thick with tall green grass, whispering to each other as she passed. It had stopped raining. Her flaming red hair streamed behind her. She had no idea where she was going, but she was desperate to get there.

On the train, her boyfriend stood silently amongst the others. Someone went for the conductor, asking for help. The police would be called. It's illegal to run off trains between stops, apparently. He stood where she had. Leaned against the window, and strained to see a hint of red amongst all the green.

EXPERIENTIAL

One of us has been invited to a party. A girl she works with is DJing there and she has put our names on a list. We walk up to the venue and it is definitely a 'club', complete with big, angry-looking bouncers, a velvet rope, a queue of anxious and excited-looking people, everything. It looks like the kind of place that was once a music hall and was later converted when the word 'crisis' was the last on anyone's mind. Apparently, super club Pacha used to be there.

We walk in and say we are on the guest list and are given a little receipt that says we get two free drinks or, wait, maybe three. Two shots and one long drink... and a bunch of other little tear-off tickets, for what I can't work out.

When we get inside it is heaving and on stage is what looks like a band, only they don't actually seem to be playing anything. Some house-y music is playing, and they, this make-believe band, looking like their average age is about seventeen, are mucking about on instruments, a drum machine and other electronic things. But whatever they are doing is making no real difference to the soundscape we are hearing.

The other girls I'm with must be thinking the same thing, because we are all staring at the stage with strained confused expressions. Finally one of us says,

'Are they actually playing anything...?'

We look back to the stage, still none the wiser.

'Drink?' the other girl asks. We walk quickly to the bar in unanimous agreement. I notice something. The bar only serves Jack Daniel's. This strikes me as strange; not the strangest, but there is something else about it that is odd, and I can't, I'm not sure what it...?

The bartender serves me a double Jack and Coke that tastes like a triple. It would be more accurate to call it a Jack Daniel's with a Coke top (dash of Coke? Misting?). Does he smile when he takes my drink ticket? I can't remember, but I notice his Jack

Daniel's T-shirt. And the other bartenders' Jack Daniel's T-shirts, and the bar shelf with light-up Jack Daniel's logos. Still not so weird, brands pay for stuff these days, normal. After all, I am living in a city where the central metro station was renamed 'Vodafone Sol'.

I take a generous sip from my Jack and Coke, in a tall Jack Daniel's glass, and the band... the band... no, wait, the instruments... they are *all* branded.

There is a Jack Daniel's drum kit and a Jack Daniel's keyboard and a cute indie girl photographer taking pictures of it all, wearing black skinny jeans and a Jack Daniel's T-shirt.

We go on a wander and find ourselves in a line to get a group picture, and just as we are about to have it taken I get it: the pictures will be printed for us to keep... OK, cute, and then what? Projected on the wall? Why? I look at the stream of pictures projected of others at the party, wearing variations of Jack Daniel's T-shirts, and over them a hashtag for a certain whiskey...

We are thinking about getting another drink and notice our tickets get us other things. A T-shirt? With what on it? Let me guess...

We see a guy dressed up like a beekeeper... pouring shots... free? OK, great! Sure!

'What's with the outfit?' one of us asks. He sprays some dry ice out of a little machine and laughs. I ask if he likes the job. He says yes. We get shots, honey-flavoured... right. We are running out of little tickets.

Above our heads TV screens with Jack Daniel's logos, strobe lighting in a variety of florescent hues. I realise we are now waiting in a queue, for what? Free customising of our T-shirts. What... really? One of the girls says all they are doing is adding eyelets, and decides against it (smart move). I walk over to check out the 'customising 'in action.

On a long table are two rent-a-hipsters, one in each gender.

A broad-shouldered bearded guy in a buttoned-up check shirt taking T-shirts into a little machine that adds studs, and a midriff-baring, skinny-jeans-wearing peroxide blonde with a pixie cut, adding eyelets and cutting off sleeves. I find this hilarious.

'This is nuts. I'm going for it, let them customise my branding,' I say, and one of my friends decides to stay with me.

We are looking at the room around us, getting dizzy from all the Jack Daniel's logos on display, when a very petite girl beside me says something.

I look down to her; she grumbles it again. I explain in broken Spanish that I don't speak Spanish. She then tells me in perfect English:

'This is a line, I have been waiting here for one hour, you can't just walk in.'

I have lived in London for eighteen years and a Spanish girl is schooling *me* on queuing. She is calm and yet quietly furious. She must have been thinking this for the last fifteen minutes, because it has been at least that long that we have been in the line.

'You have been waiting here for an hour to have your Jack Daniel's T-shirt customised?'

I look down at the black T-shirt she is proudly clutching to herself.

'Yes,' she says huffily.

'OK,' I say, 'sorry…'

My friend adds,
'It's all right, we're not bothered really.'

We walk away. I look back at the long queue incredulously. OK…

OK, that girl has been waiting *an hour* for her piece of live-in advertising to be studded by a rent-a-hipster. And she isn't even embarrassed to admit it. What is wrong? What is wrong here?!

Now the alcohol is starting to hit, and I am feeling a bit delirious, and concerned, concerned that no one in the room seems to be aware they are in a living breathing commercial, a dancing all-drinking immersive advertising experience. And no one looks bothered by it. People are enjoying it.

And the worst part is, it feels like someone in youth marketing has gone, 'What do young people like? Electro bands! Hashtags! Printed photographs! Instagram! Customising! Who is cool enough to customise? A peroxide blonde and a guy with a really bushy beard! Now let's put it all together, add shitloads of alcohol, disco lights, and chuck a bunch of logos over it!'

Does no one else find this wrong?

I make jokes about this to my friend Jenny, who does find it funny but is perhaps not feeling quite as disturbed by it as me. I need to tell people what's going on. I need to tell... I notice a brunette with perfectly straight indie fringe standing next to me.

'Hey!' I half-shout at her over the blaring music (I don't even think it occurs to me she won't speak English).

She smiles at me. I smile back at her and say, 'This is totally weird, right?'

Her smile wavers. 'What's weird?'

'This event. This party. This scene.'

'Why?'

'All the branding. I mean, I get it: sponsorship, sponsored events, sponsored festivals, logos in bars even. But this is too much, this is weird. In London, where I live, people would find this really uncool. In Berlin, where I lived before that, no one would want to be here, this wouldn't happen. I mean, it's over the top, don't you think?'

I'm rambling, she hasn't said anything. Her smile has tightened across her face until she's almost grimacing. She says to me sharply, 'But everyone here knows it's a Jack Daniel's event. Actually, I work for Jack Daniel's marketing.'

Now, a normal person would have left the conversation now, but for some reason I persist.

'Yeah, OK, cool, but what I'm saying is…you work there, but you seem cool. I mean, I get that this is your job or whatever, so you have to support it, or pretend that you do, but come on, I mean, seriously,' – I gesture around me – 'this is heavy-handed brand promotion. Right?'

She is not nodding. She is glaring… at me.

I realise… I am in my first party in Madrid… and I have made my first enemy.

The next day, the hangover I have is legendary. My great-grandchildren will tell their children about it as a bedtime story. It is absolutely mythical. The black T-shirt with the white logo stays in the back of my shelf.

I swear to myself…

I will never drink Jack Daniel's again.

TOWER

She suggests going on a walk. We walk up so many stairs I think I may pass out, but when we make it to the top the view is more than worth it. She tells me, 'It's so beautiful. I love it here.'

She asks me if I see the tower. I don't. She points it out and tells me that there is a number you can text. If you love someone, if there is someone you like you can text this number and then a big heart will appear in lights on the screen of the tower.

What? Are you serious? Yes. She looks wistful.

'So if you come here and you are in love, you can do it. I can give you the number.'

I suggest that maybe you could appreciate the heart projection just for the sake of it. Or maybe with a friend, maybe it doesn't have to be some big romantic expression. I'm teasing her a little. But she isn't up for making light of it, so we walk on.

Yesterday, after we three make it up to a castle that is not open because of construction work (even castles need to close for maintenance), we turn and take in the view of all these medieval houses and onwards to the hills, and the church bells are ringing like mad.

I like him because he is a warm kind of quiet. Not shy, but never feeling a constant need to talk. I like her because she seems to say exactly what she feels, when she feels, as she feels it, without a filter because why do we need filters anyway?

We make our way to a little café and order drinks and schnitzel and I go to find the ladies' room, and when I come back and walk to our table in my riding trousers and brown leather boots she nods at me appreciatively and says, 'You're really sexy.'

And the thing is there is nothing sexual in the statement; it is said simply as fact. And I say thank you somewhat awkwardly and she says,

'It's important to say these things when you think them.' And we all agree.

CONTROLLED

Trains in Germany are never late. You can set your clocks by them. But on this icy minus-ten day, standing alone on an empty platform, every ten minutes my train was announced as later still. Ten minutes late became twenty minutes, became thirty. I was freezing. I was so cold all I could think about was how cold I was, and then I saw them.

Two tall police officers, approaching up the stairs with no sense of urgency, talking to one another. I kept focused on the display board, hoping there would be no further delays. As they drew closer I still didn't think they could be coming over to me until there they were, asking – politely, I should add – where was I going?

'Leipzig.'

In the pop quiz I wasn't aware I was taking, this was the first wrong answer. Why was I going from this platform when I should be going the other direction? Ah, because of a problem with the trains, I had to go change at the main station. OK, fine. Was I living in Dresden? No? OK. Did I understand German?

I smiled. This struck me as funny, as it was in German that we were speaking.

'English?' he said sharply.

So in German I replied, 'Yes, perhaps better we speak in English.'

And then he asked:

'Can I see your passport?'

In Germany, the police have the right to stop anyone at any time and ask to see their ID. If you're a foreigner this means carrying your passport. You hear that you can carry a driver's licence or a photocopy of your passport, but this isn't true. By law you must carry your passport with you at all times. In Berlin, many foreigners I know that live there don't.

I didn't feel great about this random check, but instinct told me to be polite and cooperate. That way it would be over with quickly.

They both peered closely at my passport, passing it back and forth between them a few times. The first started to bend it back at the sides. Then he flipped it to the front page, inspecting the biometric chip. He flipped it to the other side, gave me a long look that suggested comparing me to the picture within it. He asked, suspiciously,

'You were born in Washington DC?'

'Yes.'

'You also have American passport?'

'I used to but it expired. I moved to Europe as a teenager; since then I haven't needed it.'

I am used to official people being confused about dual citizenship. A lot of people, even people working in customs and passport control, don't get it. I would be happy to explain. What I didn't expect was for him to change his tone and ask sharply:

'Why do you have this document?'

'Sorry? I don't understand.'

I really didn't.

'How do you have this passport?'

'My father is English.'

This also appeared to be the wrong answer.

'You do not have an American passport?'

'I did. I stopped using it. I have lived in Europe since I was a teenager.'

He nodded, unconvinced, and passed my passport back to his colleague who flipped through the pages at various speeds, stopped, played the front page back and forth in the light, checking the hologram, took out a small magnifying glass and scanned the small print.

What were they looking for? Why were they doing this? What would they do next? How long would they keep it?

And then I understood...

They think my passport is fake!

The guy who had been inspecting it now walked off a couple metres, calling someone on his phone. I watched with concern as he walked away further. His colleague kept close to me. I asked him, 'Is there a problem?'

'No. Don't worry, nothing is wrong.' Inexplicably, he was smiling.

The sentiment seemed to be it was silly for me to be concerned. As if them checking my passport didn't suggest that they thought something with it might be wrong.

Ten minutes later I was given it back with no apology or explanation as to why it had been taken and inspected. The policemen walked to the end of the platform, staring at me as they lit their cigarettes, before eventually looking away...

and then finally, mercifully, my train came.

HOME

When I spoke to you earlier, there were all these things I wanted to tell you. But I got a bit scrambled talking to you. Just hearing your voice was overwhelming; hearing your voice like that, relaxed, pausing from the book you were reading, had a resonance, a richness that made me want to lie down with it and you.

So I rambled about liking being here, and didn't ask enough questions about your day, and then didn't quite know what to ask or say so probably repeated myself. Frustrated, I murmured,

'The problem is talking to you makes me want to see you.'

But I was too quiet and you didn't hear, so you said,

'Did you say I really miss you?'

Which was similar but not what I said. I couldn't repeat it. What I meant was the more I heard you, the more real you became and the more I craved you, the touch and taste of you. The harder it was for me to be away.

Last night I spoke about you to her. I was overcome with so many thoughts I wanted to say and to write to you. I wanted to say crazy things. I wanted to say I felt as if I could have told you that you are not just the one that I love. That you are the only one I have ever loved.

I did not say any of those things. Instead I told her that you had become my 'home'.

She said it was normal to make your lover 'home' when your home felt uncertain.

In Ghana, I told my parents I felt homesick, but when I said that I didn't mean I wanted to come back to Berlin or to London. I meant that I was sick of being in a place that was not home.

I'm not sure what home is anymore. When people ask me if I miss America, if I want to go back, the place I spent seventeen years of my life holds no pull for me, has ceased to be real.

Berlin feels like a home I've moved on from. London is the home I am forever questioning.

You are my home now. You are the only home that I have.

ACKNOWLEDGEMENTS

Thanks (in no particular order): Clive Birnie, Adrian Gillott, Femi Martin, Chris Singleton, Matt Macdonald, Dan Simpson, Keith Jarrett, Gary Hartley, Tina Sederholm, Nicola Browning, Mette Rietzel, Michael Haeflinger, Katinka Kraft, Jonas McCloud, Naruna Kaplan De Macedo, Jenny Edwards, Katja Hoffman, Elaine Cassetti, Monica Rief, Abbey Quin, Simon Quin, Salena Godden, Benjamin Macoy, Monica Rief and to you for being there, for being here, for listening and for reading.

'Real', 'Clarification' and 'Dear Straight Girl' were previously published in *Flicker and Spark: A Contemporary Queer Anthology of Spoken Word and Poetry*, edited by Regie Cabico and Brittany Fonte.